EARTH FIGURED OUT

Life Cycles

Nancy Dickmann

Cavendish
Square

New York

Published in 2016 by Cavendish Square Publishing, LLC
243 5th Avenue, Suite 136, New York, NY 10016

Website: cavendishsq.com

This publication represents the opinions and views of the author based on his or her personal
experience, knowledge, and research. The information in this book serves as a general guide only.
The author and publisher have used their best efforts in preparing this book and disclaim liability
rising directly or indirectly from the use and application of this book.

CPSIA Compliance Information: Batch #CW16CSQ

All websites were available and accurate when this book was sent to press.

Cataloging-in-Publication Data

Dickmann, Nancy.
Life cycles / by Nancy Dickmann.
p. cm. — (Earth figured out)
Includes index.
ISBN 978-1-5026-0864-2 (hardcover) ISBN 978-1-5026-0862-8 (paperback)
ISBN 978-1-5026-0865-9 (ebook)
1. Life cycles (Biology) — Juvenile literature. I. Dickmann, Nancy. II. Title.
QH501.D53 2016
571.8—d23

Produced for Cavendish Square by Calcium
Editors: Sarah Eason and Harriet McGregor
Designer: Paul Myerscough

The photographs in this book are used by permission and through the courtesy of:
Alex James Bramwell/Shutterstock.com, cover; Insides: Shutterstock: Chris Alcock 26–27, Nick
Biemans 29b, Bluedogroom 4–5, David Evison 1, 18–19, Eric Gevaert 20–21, Inlovepai 8–9,
Brian A. Jackson 6t, Sebastian Kaulitzki 15b, Kkaplin 10–11, Leungchopan 12–13, Monkey
Business Images 13tr, 14–15, Krzysztof Odziomek 27t, Paladin12 6–7, PCHT 21b, Rawpixel
16, Villiers Steyn 23, Taiftin 4, TessarTheTegu 24–25, Tulpahn 9t, Dennis van de Water 28–29,
Wildnerdpix 11, K.A.Willis 18b, Roger Wissmann 22, Matej Ziak 25b, ZouZou 16–17.

Printed in the United States of America

Contents

What Is a Life Cycle?

All living things, from tiny insects to tall trees, have a life cycle. Some life cycles can last for just a few days, and others can go on for thousands of years. A living **organism** can begin life in many different ways. For example, it can be born, like humans are. Some living things hatch from eggs, and others sprout from **seeds**. A few organisms, such as hydra, start life when they grow on a part of their parent's body.

Once an organism begins its life, it grows and changes. After a while, it will be ready to make its own young. It might lay eggs, produce seeds, or give birth. Some living things produce young only once before they die. Others can go on **reproducing** for years. In the end, living things will die. They may be killed by a **predator**, or die of illness or old age. Often, their offspring survive to continue the life cycle.

The pine cones on this tree each contain many small seeds, which can grow into new trees.

During their life cycle, most living things do certain things, called life processes. For example, all living things grow. They must take in and use food, and get rid of waste. They also reproduce, which means making more living things of the same type.

After hatching, this baby snake will grow and develop until it is able to lay its own eggs.

How Plants Grow

The life cycle of many types of plants starts with a seed. A seed contains the beginnings of a new plant. It also has food that the new plant will need. When a seed absorbs water, the process of sprouting begins. The outer seed case splits, and roots develop. The roots extend into the soil and take up water and **nutrients**.

The first shoots and leaves grow upward, and they use sunlight to make food for the plant. More and more leaves grow, and the plant becomes taller and thicker. Once it is grown, it will be ready to make seeds of its own.

Some types of plants do not grow from seeds. For example, a potato produces tiny sprouts. If these are cut off and planted, they will grow into new potatoes. A strawberry plant sends out special stems called "runners" across the ground. These runners work their way into the ground and form roots for new plants.

Seeds can travel away from their parent plant in different ways. These dandelion seeds are very light and shaped so that they can travel on the wind.

EARTH FIGURED OUT

Plants need water, air, sunlight, warmth, and nutrients in order to grow. Plants combine the energy from sunlight with water and gases in the air to make their own food. This process is called **photosynthesis**. Water is also needed to keep plant stems strong.

These seedlings have sprouted from seeds beneath the surface of the soil. Once the store of food inside the seeds is used up, the seeds will break up and disappear.

Flowers, Fruits, and Pollination

The life cycle continues when a fully grown plant makes its own seeds. Many plants have flowers with both male and female parts. The male parts produce **pollen**, which is like sticky dust. In order to make seeds, the pollen must be transferred to the female parts of a plant.

Pollen can be blown from one plant to another by the wind. However, many plants rely on insects, birds, and bats to spread their pollen. Their flowers produce a sweet liquid called nectar. When animals come to the flower to drink the nectar, they brush against the male parts and pollen sticks to their bodies. When they fly to another plant, the pollen brushes onto its female parts. Once this happens, the flower can make seeds. Often the seeds develop inside a fruit, such as an apple.

EARTH FIGURED OUT

Plants have different ways of attracting insects, birds, and other pollinators. They provide a "reward" in the form of nectar or pollen to eat. Some animals are attracted by a flower's bright colors. Others may like its scent—even if it smells disgusting to humans! Some flowers are specially shaped to form a landing platform for flying insects.

Nectar is an important food for bees, butterflies, and many other animals. Nectar is sugary and full of energy.

Some seeds are spread when an animal eats a plant's fruit. The seeds come out later in their waste.

PLANT LIFE CYCLES—FIGURED OUT!

Many scientists believe that the oldest living individual plant is a bristlecone pine tree in the United States, which is

5,065

years old.

A type of palm called the Coco-de-mer produces the largest seeds of any plant. They can be almost

20

inches (50 centimeters) across and weigh as much as 66 pounds (30 kilograms)!

The record for the largest single flower belongs to the *Rafflesia arnoldii*, which produces flowers that are up to

3

feet (91 cm) across and weigh up to 15 pounds (7 kg). The *Titan arum* plant produces enormous clusters of tiny flowers, which can be 12 feet (3.7 meters) high and weigh as much as 170 pounds (77 kg)!

The tallest type of tree on Earth is the coastal redwood, found on the West Coast of the United States. The tallest one ever found was

379 feet (115 m) tall. That's as tall as a thirty-five-story building!

A seed can stay dormant for a long time before sprouting. Scientists believe that the oldest seed ever to sprout was **1,288** years old.

An avocado has just one seed. Most apples have between 2 and 15 seeds. A single strawberry has about **200** seeds.

Human Life Cycles

A human baby starts with the joining of two **cells** inside the mother. During the nine months that it stays in the **uterus**, it grows and changes. Its organs and other body parts develop. When the baby is born, it is still helpless. During childhood, a baby grows and learns. Usually, by the time it is twelve years old, a child will weigh more than ten times its birth weight. He or she will be able to speak, read, write, and do complex tasks.

Around the age of twelve, boys and girls go through a phase called puberty. This is the stage when a child's body changes to look more like an adult. Inside the body, changes are happening to make it possible to have children.

During adulthood, humans stop growing, and many of them have their own children. In old age, some body parts no longer work as well as they used to. Eventually, all humans will die.

EARTH FIGURED OUT

Your body is made up of tiny building blocks called cells. Many of these cells are constantly dying and being replaced by new ones. The cells lining your stomach might live only for a few days, while skin cells might last for a month. Some cells, such as nerve cells, last a lifetime.

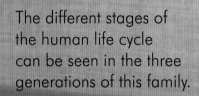
The different stages of the human life cycle can be seen in the three generations of this family.

Babies quickly learn to sit, crawl, and walk. When they are born they can't move around or feed themselves, but that soon changes as they grow.

Human Reproduction

A woman's body contains special cells called eggs, and a man produces cells called sperm. When an egg and a sperm join, an **embryo** is formed. This tiny clump of cells attaches to the wall of the woman's uterus. Then it begins to grow and develop. The cells divide to form new cells, and soon the cells start to change. For example, some will become blood cells, some will be bone cells, and some will be skin cells.

After about three weeks, the embryo's heart begins to pump blood. By the time the embryo is ten weeks old, nearly all of its organs are completely formed. At this stage, it is called a **fetus**. Within another few weeks, the fingers and toes are formed. The fetus continues to grow and develop. After about nine months inside the mother's body, it is born.

A child might get its father's hair color and its mother's eye color.

EARTH FIGURED OUT

Every person has many different physical **traits**: for example, they might be tall, with brown hair and blue eyes, and be right-handed. These traits are controlled by the **genes** that have been passed down by the person's parents. A child has a mixture of genes from both parents, so their traits are usually a mixture, too.

During the time that a baby is in the uterus, it gets everything it needs, including food and oxygen, from its mother.

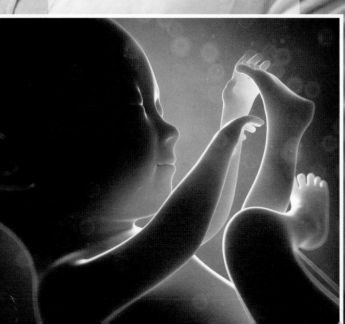

HUMAN BEINGS—FIGURED OUT!

The oldest person to ever live was a Frenchwoman named Jeanne Calment. She died in 1997 at the age of **122**.

The most common hair color in the world is black, and the most common eye color is brown. Only around **1 to 2** percent of the world's population has red hair, and about 2 percent has green eyes.

Between **5** percent and **30** percent of people are left-handed.

In the United States in 1911, the average number of children a woman would have during her life was 3.4. By 2011, that had dropped to **1.9** children per woman.

Although men can father children at any age, most women find it difficult to become pregnant after the age of around 45. The average age of a woman having her first child in the United States is 26. The oldest known mother was nearly **67** years old when she gave birth to twin boys.

The human life cycle begins when two cells merge. Scientists believe that there are around **37.2 trillion** cells in an adult human body.

Animal Reproduction

Humans are **mammals**, and many other mammals reproduce in a similar way. One or more fetuses grow in the mother's uterus until they are ready to be born. Some mammals, such as cats, are pregnant for a shorter time and have more babies. Others, such as elephants, are pregnant for longer.

Some other animals produce young in completely different ways. Birds lay eggs and then sit on them until they are ready to hatch. Inside the egg, a baby bird slowly takes shape. Many reptiles also lay eggs, although most of them do not take care of the eggs until they hatch. Nearly all amphibians, and some types of fish, also lay eggs.

A sea turtle lays up to two hundred eggs in the sand, then returns to the sea, leaving the eggs behind. When they hatch, the babies must make their own way to the water.

A newborn kangaroo is small and not well developed. It climbs into its mother's pouch to drink milk and grow for several more months.

Some animals, including humans and elephants, usually give birth to a single baby at a time. Others, such as mice or fish, might give birth to many young, often several times in one year. Animals that have fewer babies can take care of them and keep them safe until they are ready to survive on their own. Animals that have many offspring cannot raise them as carefully. Many of the young will die, but at least a few will survive to maintain the life cycle.

Raising Young

A human child often lives with its parents for eighteen years or more. It relies on its parents to provide food and protection. In the animal kingdom, this is very unusual. Many baby animals have to take care of themselves, and very few stay with their parents for more than a few years.

In some species, such as penguins, the mother and father work together to care for the babies. Other animal mothers, such as polar bears, must do it by themselves. Some types of animals, such as lions and elephants, live in groups. All the adult females in a group will help take care of the babies.

Animal parents have many different ways of keeping their animals safe and traveling with them. Some fish carry their babies in their mouths. Wolf spiders carry dozens of tiny spiderlings on their backs. Many baby monkeys use their strong fingers to cling to their mother's fur.

EARTH FIGURED OUT

Animal parents often find food for their young, and some parents actually produce it. All female mammals have mammary glands, which produce milk.

The milk contains fat, protein, sugars, and other nutrients that the baby needs. The baby drinks milk until its body is ready to digest other types of food.

A young orangutan depends on its mother for food and transportation for the first two years of its life.

These baby sun birds will be brought food by their parents until they are big enough to take care of themselves.

ANIMAL LIFE CYCLES—FIGURED OUT!

Some animals live an incredibly long time. One giant tortoise was thought to be **250** years old when it died. Scientists believe that a type of reptile called the tuatara can live for more than 200 years.

A termite queen can lay 30,000 eggs in a single day, and about **250 million** eggs in her lifetime. However, that's nothing compared to the ocean sunfish, which can produce 300 million eggs at a time!

The vervain hummingbird lays the smallest egg of any bird species. The egg is less than **0.39** inches (1 cm) long and weighs 0.0128 ounces (0.36 g). The biggest egg belongs to the ostrich. It can weigh more than 5 pounds (2.3 kg).

The African elephant stays pregnant for longer than any other mammal: about

22 months. The mammal with the shortest pregnancy is the Virginia opossum, at just 12 or 13 days.

Most of the milk we drink comes from cows. A dairy cow can produce around

8 gallons (30 liters) of milk each day.

The egg of a kiwi bird can weigh up to

25 percent of the mother's body weight. If a human baby were this big when it was born, it would be like giving birth to a four-year-old child!

Metamorphosis

Kittens and puppies look a lot like their parents. Some types of baby animals—including many insects—look completely different from their parents. Their bodies must go through a process called **metamorphosis** before they become adults.

Many insects are shaped a little like worms or caterpillars when they hatch from eggs. This stage in the life cycle is called a **larva**. The larva eats and grows and, sometimes, it sheds its stiff outer skin if the skin gets too small. Once a larva is big enough, it enters a new stage and is called a **pupa**. During this stage the insect does not eat or move around. Its body is protected by a skin or cocoon while it changes shape. After a while, an adult insect emerges.

EARTH FIGURED OUT

Insects are a well-known example of metamorphosis, but other types of animals also go through this process. Frogs start life as fish-like tadpoles, living in water and eating algae. Eventually their bodies change, and they begin a new life on land, eating insects. Some sea creatures, such as shrimp and lobsters, also go through metamorphosis.

A caterpillar is an example of a larva.
It spends its pupa stage inside a chrysalis
before emerging as an adult butterfly.

These tadpoles will soon sprout
front legs and lose their tails. They
will grow tongues and big jaws,
ready to start eating insects.

Unusual Life Cycles

In the animal kingdom, there are some weird and wonderful life cycles. Clownfish begin their life as male fish, but some become females as they grow older. Other types of fish can change from female to male. Eels change their **habitat**, not their sex. As young eels they live in freshwater rivers, but they swim to the salty ocean to give birth.

The periodical cicadas of the eastern United States are the longest-living insect on the continent. When these insects hatch from their eggs, the white, ant-like young dig into the soil. They stay underground for years, sucking liquid from the roots of plants. They grow and develop until one day, the adult cicadas all emerge creating a noisy flying swarm.

Some cicada species stay underground for thirteen years, and others stay underground for seventeen years.

EARTH FIGURED OUT

One of the most amazing animals of all is the immortal jellyfish. Scientists recently discovered that these jellyfish can reverse their life cycles. All jellyfish start as a small blob (called a polyp) before taking their adult shape. Incredibly, the immortal jellyfish can change back into a polyp when it is starving or under stress. Then it slowly grows back into an adult jellyfish—and it can do this over and over.

Orange-and-white striped clownfish live on many coral reefs.

Life Cycles on Earth

There are many different animals and plants on Earth, and they all have different life cycles, too. From seeds sprouting to eggs hatching, there are a lot of ways for living things to grow and reproduce.

Everything lives in a habitat, which could be a dry desert, a cold ocean, or even a rotting tree in a forest. Many plant and animal life cycles have developed in order to **adapt** to a habitat. For example, some cacti are able to grow very quickly. When conditions are good, they shoot up fast.

Many animals, such as bears, **hibernate** during the winter. Food is hard to find then, so by hibernating the bears use less energy. Many mother bears give birth during the hibernation period, waking up every now and then to feed or clean their cubs.

Everywhere you look, you can see life cycles in action.

28

Many plants and animals never get to complete their life cycle. They may be eaten by a predator or cut down for food. Humans can affect the life cycles of plants and animals.

When we build towns and clear farmland, we destroy or change habitats. The plants and animals that live there must adapt or move to a new habitat in order to survive.

This zebra's life cycle has been cut short, but the mother lion is teaching her cub how to hunt and survive on its own.

Glossary

adapt To change, over time, in order to survive and reproduce in a particular habitat.

cells The smallest building blocks of life. Plants and animals are made up of cells.

embryo An animal that is just starting to develop inside its mother or inside an egg or seed.

fetus An unborn baby that is more developed than an embryo. A human baby is called a fetus once it has been growing for about two months.

genes The codes inside a cell that cause particular traits, such as hair color. Genes are passed down from parents to offspring.

habitat The natural environment of an animal or plant.

hibernate To sleep through the winter in a den or burrow to save energy.

larva The young form of some types of insect before it changes into an adult. Larvae do not have wings and they look a little like worms.

mammals A group of animals that have fur or hair and that make milk to feed their babies.

metamorphosis The change in shape of some living things as they grow. A caterpillar changing into a butterfly is an example of metamorphosis.

nutrients The substances in food that a living thing needs in order to grow and stay healthy.

organism A living thing.

photosynthesis The process in which a plant uses sunlight to change water and carbon dioxide into food for itself.

pollen The sticky powder made by flowers that helps them to form seeds.

predator An animal that hunts another animal for food.

pupa The middle stage of some insect life cycles. Some insects spend their time as a pupa inside a cocoon.

reproducing Having babies.

seeds The small parts of a flowering plant that grow into new plants.

traits The characteristics that make a living thing different from others of the same type, for example, height or eye color.

uterus A sac-like organ inside a female mammal in which a fetus develops.

Further Reading

Books

Amstutz, L. J. *Investigating Plant Life Cycles.* Searchlight Books. Minneapolis, MN: Lerner Classroom, 2016.

Daniels, Patricia, Christina Wilsdon, and Jen Agresta. *Ultimate Bodypedia: An Amazing Inside-Out Tour of the Human Body.* National Geographic Kids. Washington, DC: National Geographic Children's Books, 2014.

Higgins, Nadia. *Life Science Through Infographics.* Super Science Infographics. Minneapolis, MN: Lerner Publishing Group, 2013.

Spilsbury, Louise. *Kill or Die: Extreme Life Cycles.* Extreme Biology. New York: Gareth Stevens Publishing, 2015.

Taylor, Barbara. *Slimy Spawn and Other Gruesome Life Cycles.* Disgusting and Dreadful Science. New York: Crabtree Publishing Company, 2014.

Websites

This site has information about the life cycle of butterflies, with activities and a lot of photos:
www.kidsbutterfly.org/life-cycle

The scarab beetle is a fascinating insect. You can learn about its life cycle here:
museum.unl.edu/research/entomology/Scarabs-for-Kids/ cycle.html

See how plants grow in this amazing time-lapse video:
www.pbslearningmedia.org/resource/tdc02.sci.life.colt.plantsgrow/ from-seed-to-flower

Visit this site to find links to videos about animal life cycles:
www.watchknowlearn.org/Category.aspx?CategoryID=6721

Index